LEARN TO TRACE
LETTERS
AND
NUMBERS

Practice Book For Preschoolers.
Pen Control, Count, and Color.

Thank You!

Thank you for choosing **Learn to Trace Letter and Numbers.** We hope you and your child enjoy the activities and have a lot of fun together.

If you find it helpful, please consider leaving a review to share your thoughts. Your feedback helps us improve and assists other parents in finding great resources for their kids.

Thank you once again for your support!

SCAN ME

Get Free Coloring Pages!

Dear Reader,

Thank you for choosing our book! We would love to stay connected with you and share more exciting content. As a token of our appreciation, we're offering you these FREE coloring pages filled with fun and engaging designs that your kids will love!

How to Get Your Free Coloring Pages:

• Scan the QR code below

• Enter your email address

• Receive and enjoy your free coloring pages!

We look forward to staying in touch and bringing more joy and creativity to your family! Thank you for your support!

SCAN ME

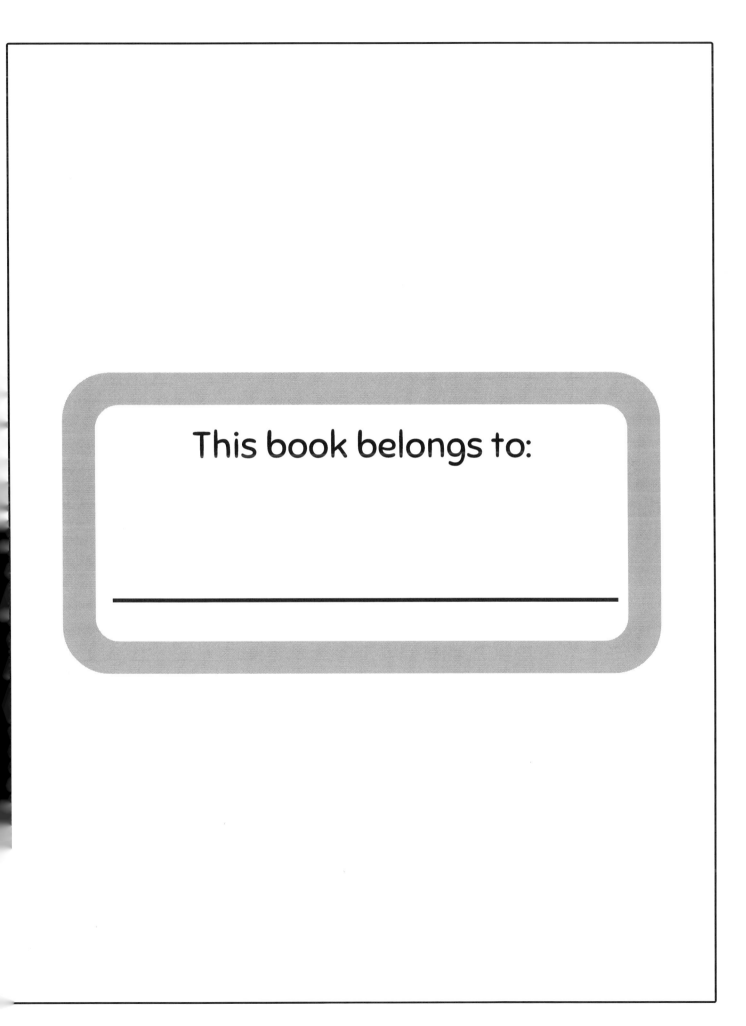

This book belongs to:

_____

Table of Contents

Pencil Control

Trace the lines in the arrow direction.

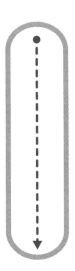   

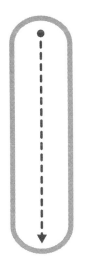 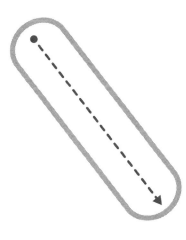  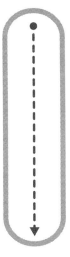

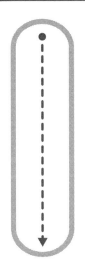 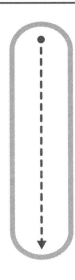 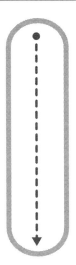 

Pencil Control

Trace the lines in the arrow direction.

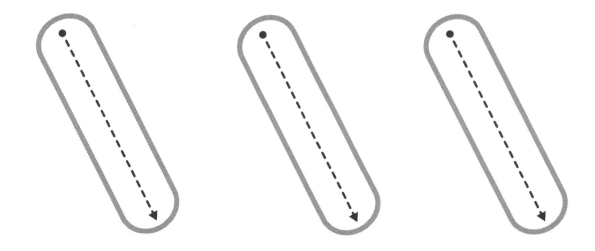

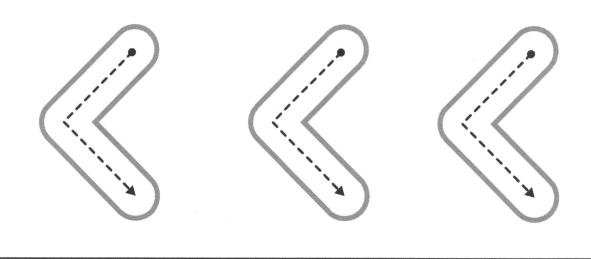

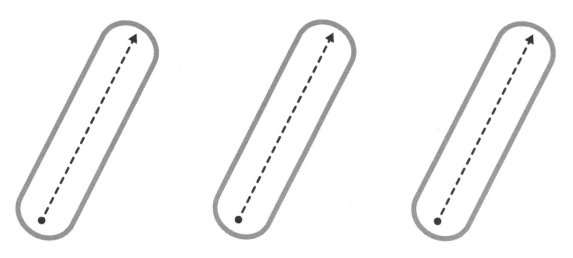

Pencil Control

Trace the lines in the arrow direction.

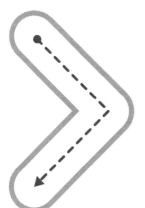 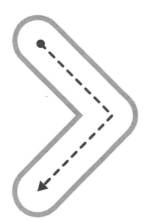 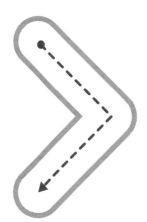

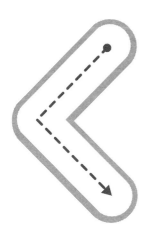 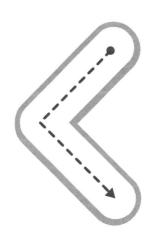 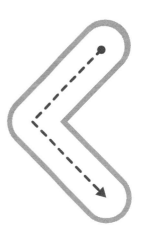

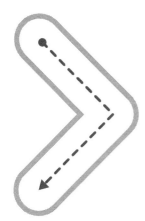 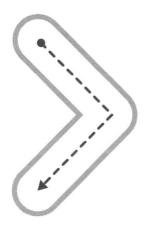 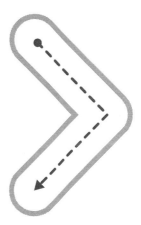

Pencil Control

Trace the lines in the arrow direction.

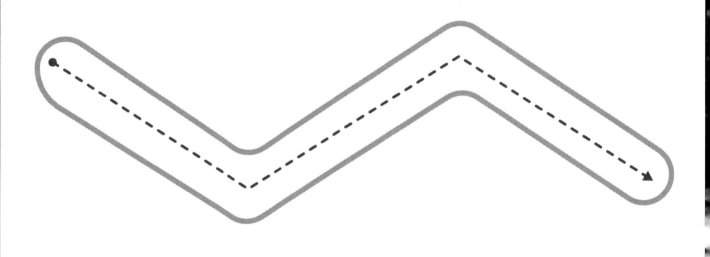

4

Pencil Control

Trace the lines in the arrow direction.

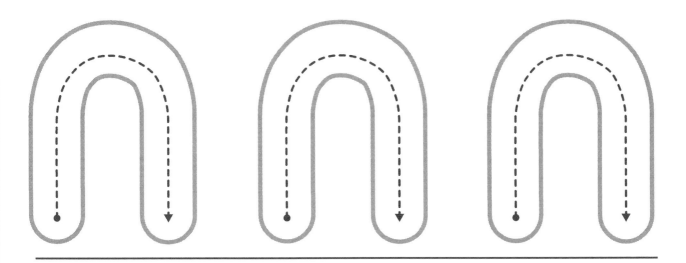

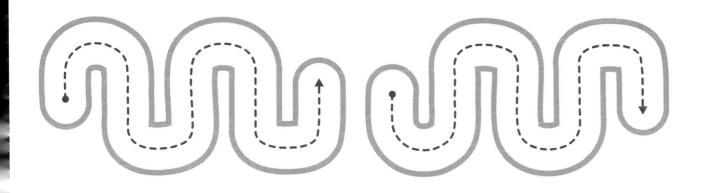

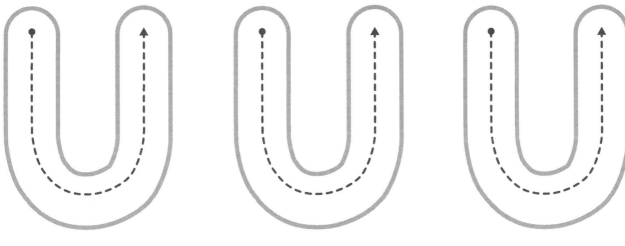

Pencil Control

Trace the lines in the arrow direction.

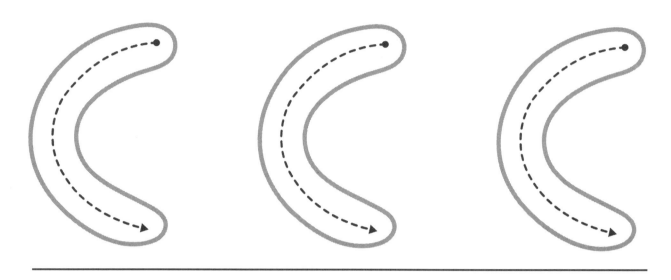

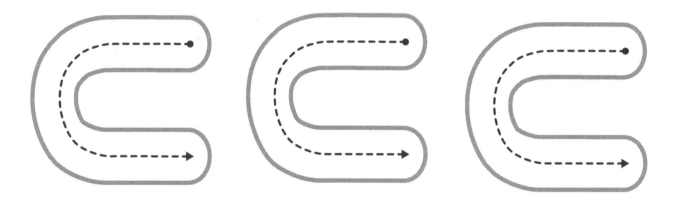

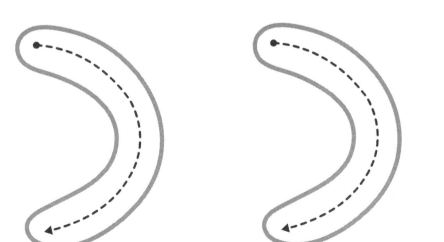

Pencil Control

Trace the lines in the arrow direction. Color the image.

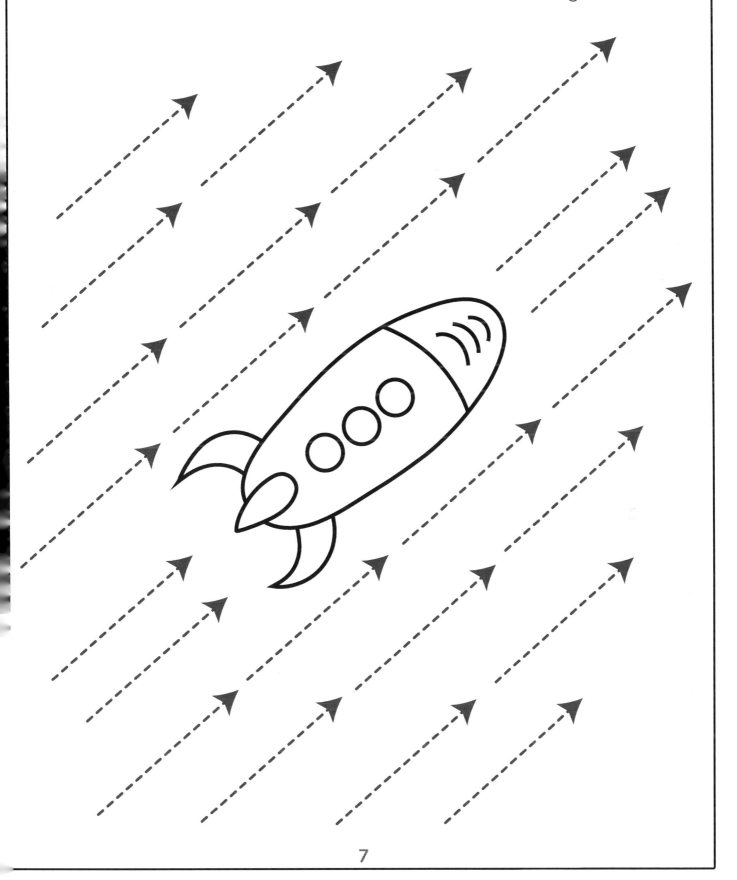

Shapes and Colors

Trace the shapes and color them.

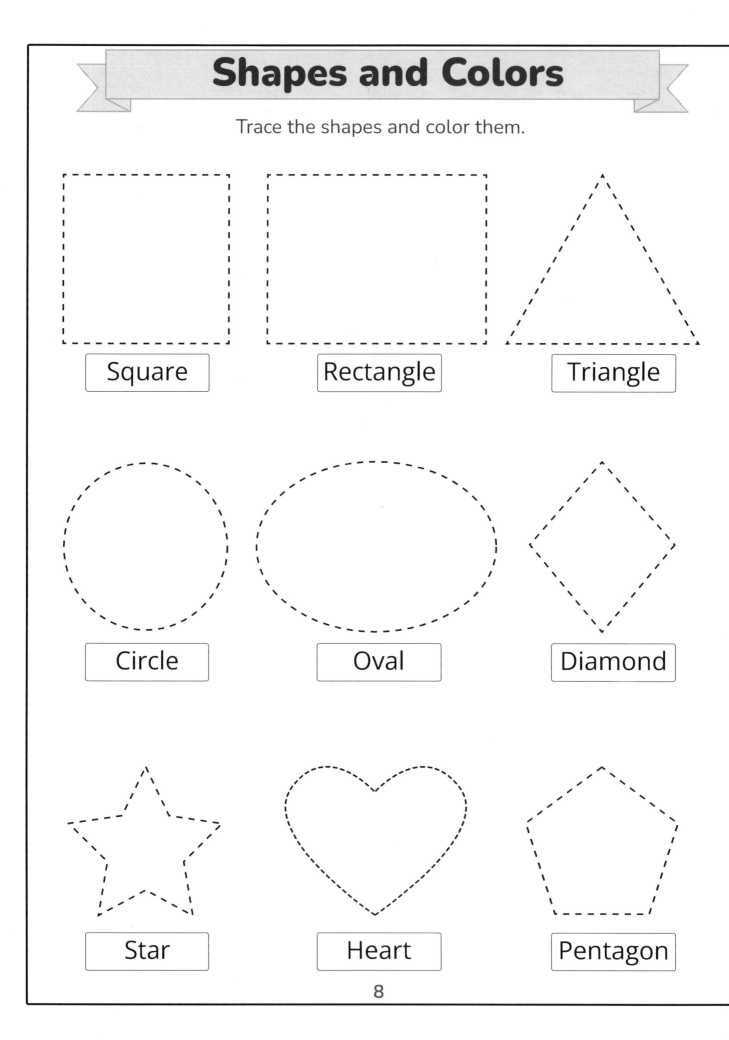

| Square | Rectangle | Triangle |

| Circle | Oval | Diamond |

| Star | Heart | Pentagon |

Shapes and Colors

Draw to complete the other half of each shape, then color as instructed.

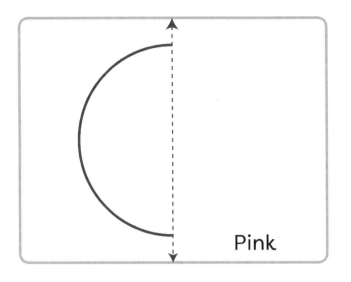

Pink

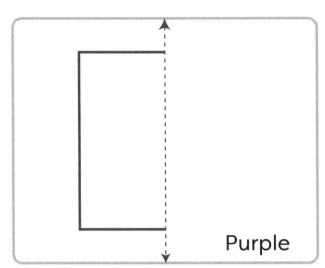

Purple

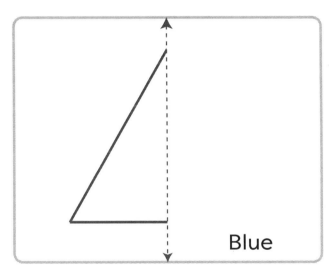

Blue

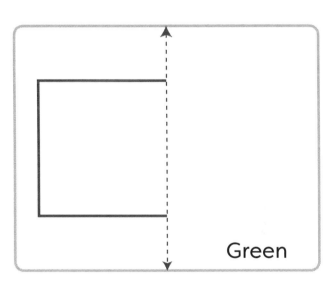

Green

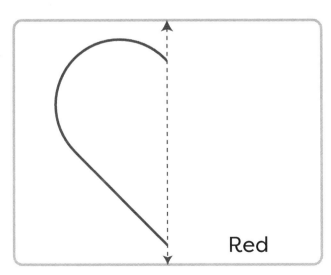

Red

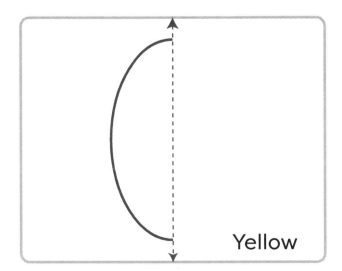

Yellow

Shapes and Colors

Draw to complete the other half of each shape, then color as instructed.

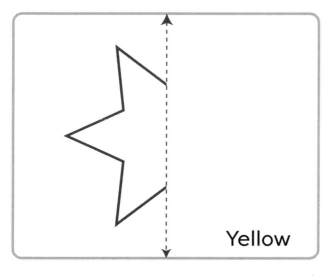

Yellow

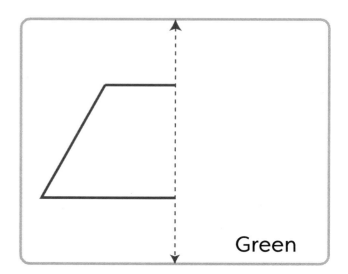

Green

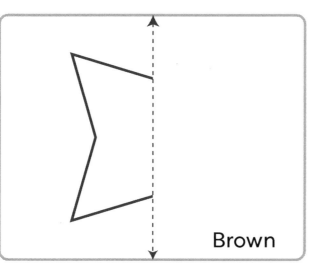

Brown

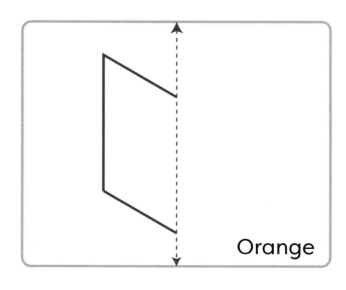

Orange

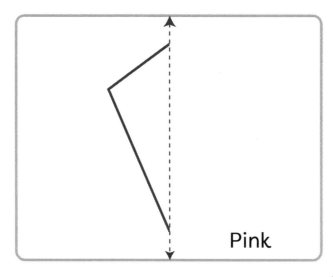

Pink

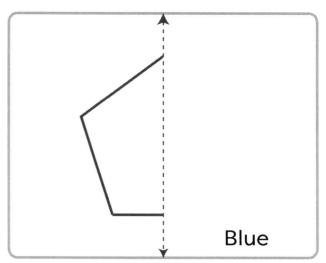

Blue

Shapes and Colors

Color the CIRCLES RED, the TRIANGLES YELLOW, and the SQUARES BLUE.

Shapes and Colors

Circles and rectangles bunnies. Follow the instructions below.

If you see a ◯ color it yellow!

If you see a ▭ color it green!

Shapes and Colors

Color by size: biggest in BLUE, medium in RED, smallest in YELLOW.

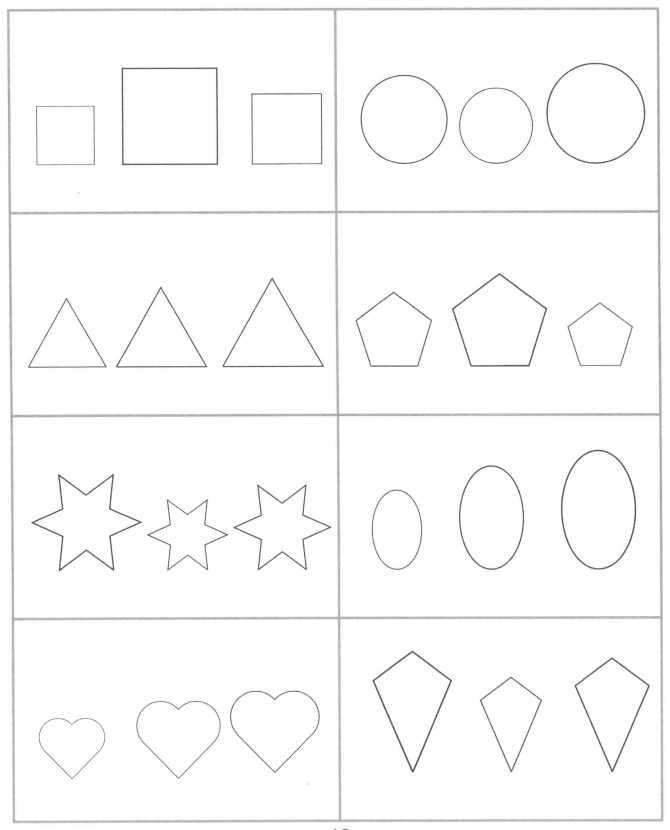

Letter Tracing

Trace and write. Then color the images.

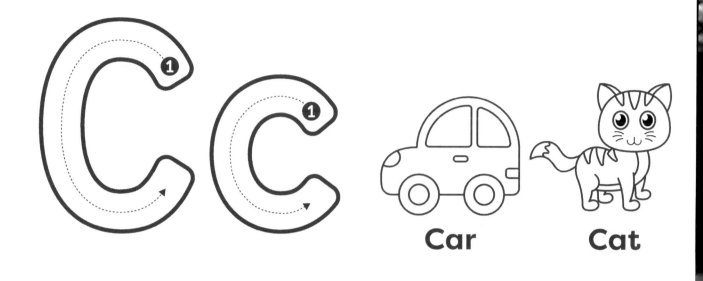

Car   Cat

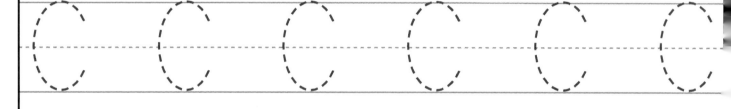

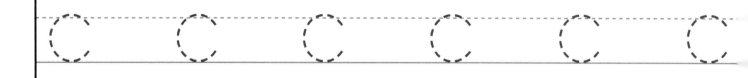

Letter Tracing

Trace and write. Then color the images.

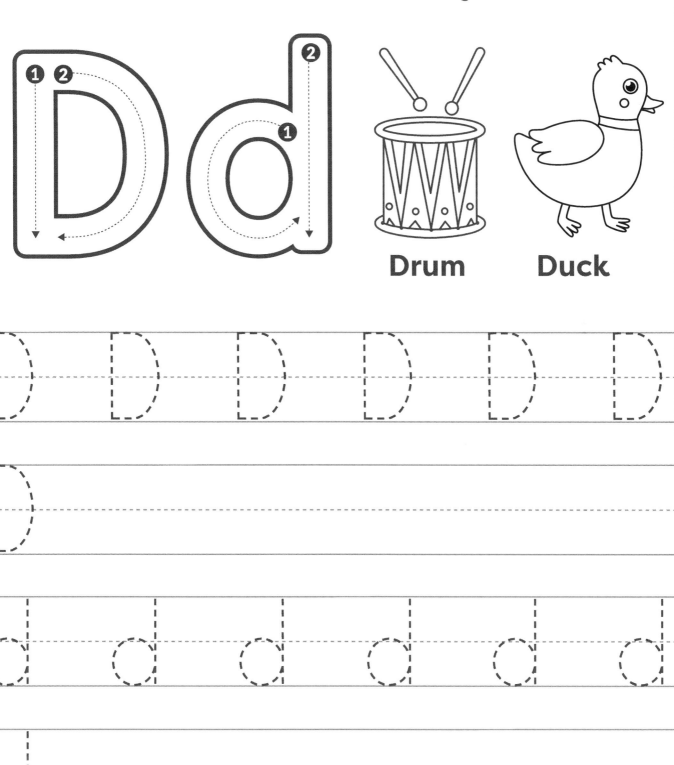

Drum

Duck

Letter Tracing

Trace and write. Then color the images.

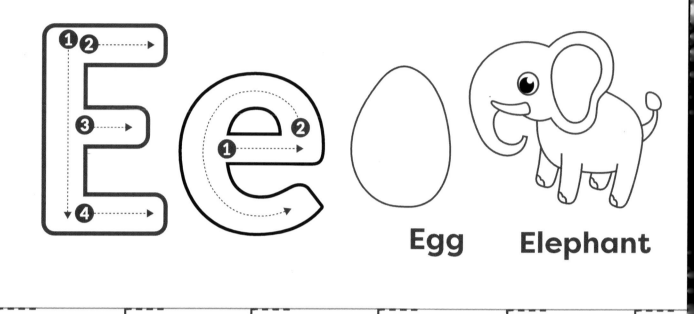

Egg   **Elephant**

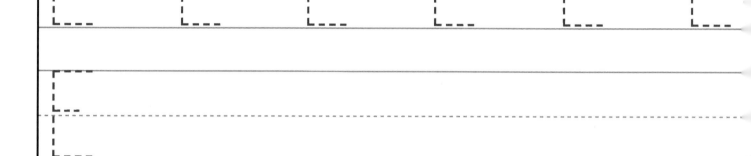

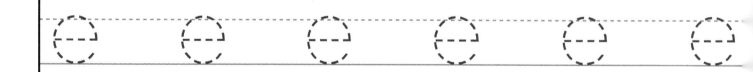

Letter Tracing

Trace and write. Then color the images.

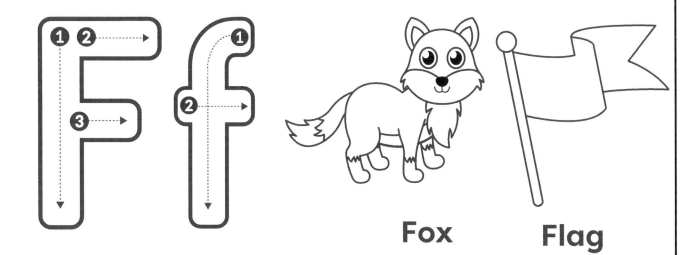

Fox   Flag

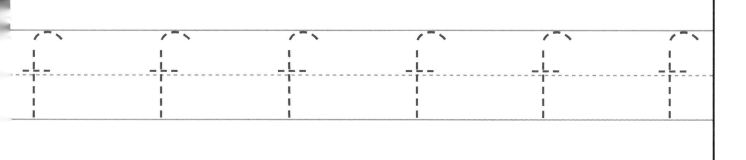

Letter Tracing

Trace and write. Then color the images.

Goat   Giraffe

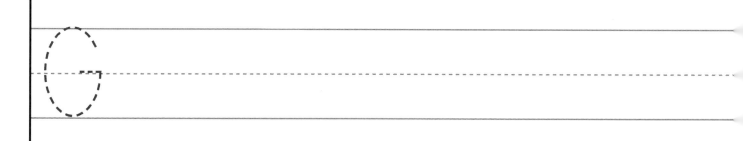

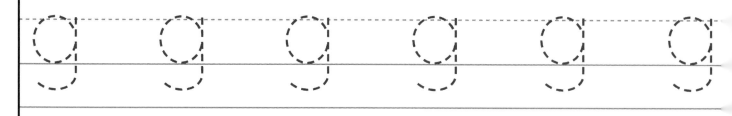

20

Letter Tracing

Trace and write. Color the images that start with the letter Hh.

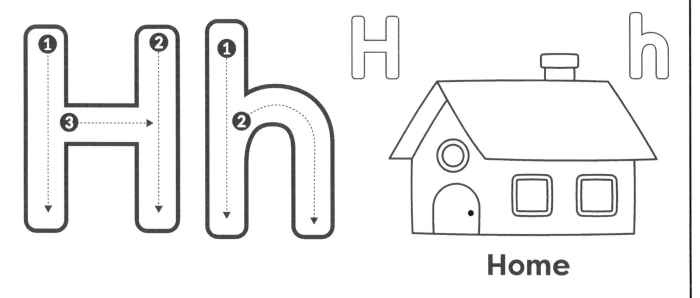

Home

Letter Tracing

Trace and write. Color the images that start with the letter Ii.

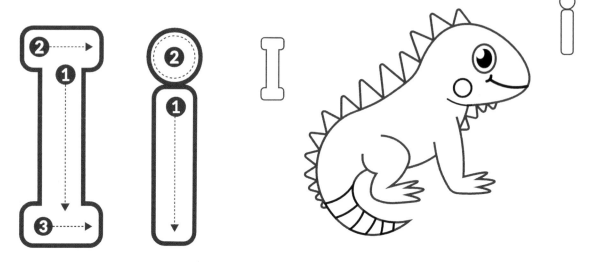

Iguana

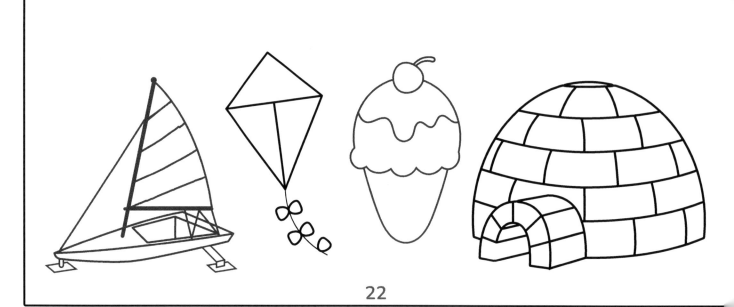

Letter Tracing

Trace and write. Color the images that start with the letter Jj.

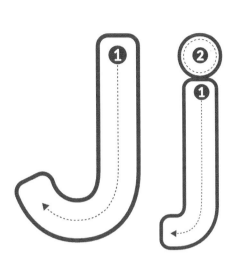 J j

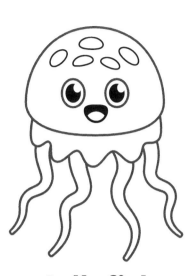

Jellyfish

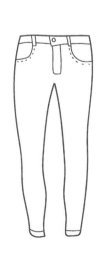 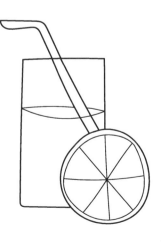  

Letter Tracing

Trace and write. Color the images that start with the letter Kk.

Kangaroo

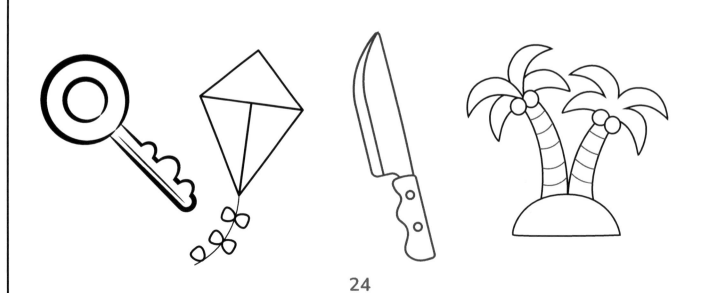

Letter Tracing

Trace and write. Color the images that start with the letter Ll.

Ladybug

Letter Tracing

Trace and write. Color the images that start with the letter Mm.

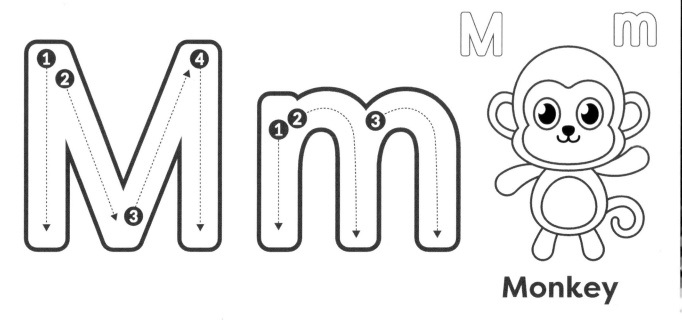

Monkey

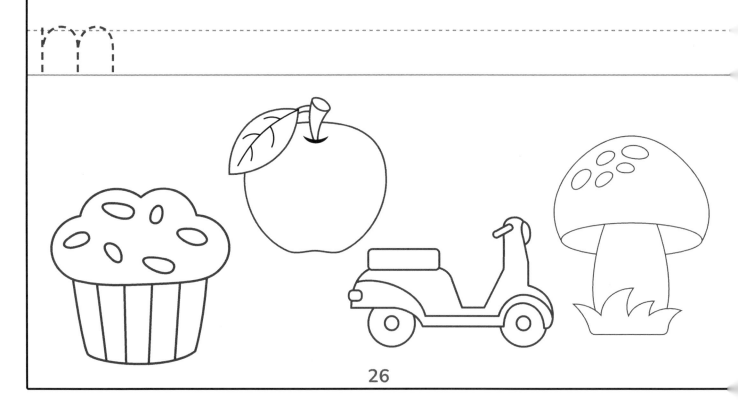

Letter Tracing

Trace the letter below. Color the images that start with the letter N. Color the circles with the letter Nn in them.

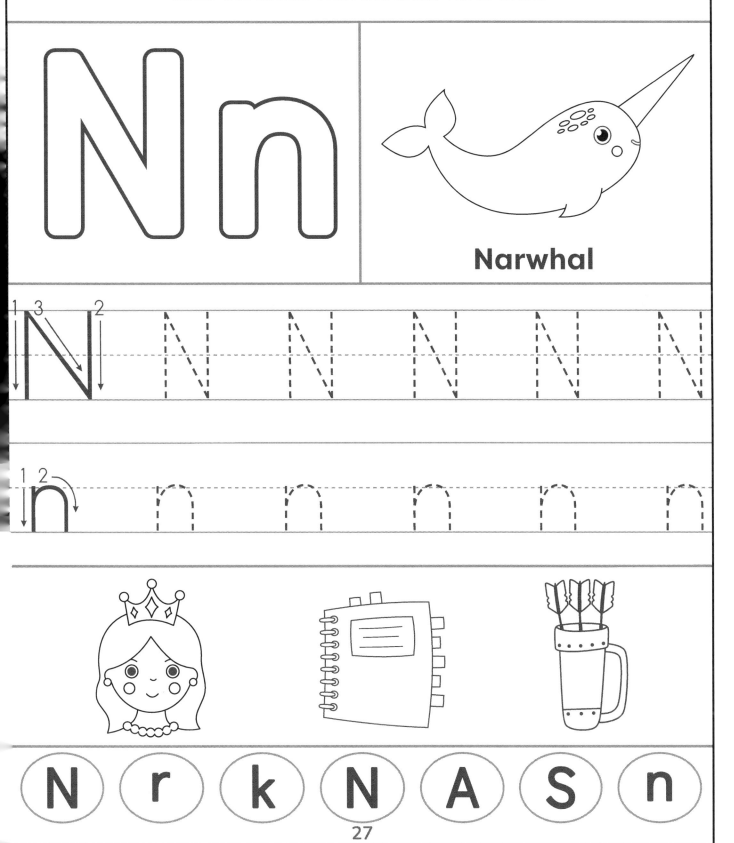

Narwhal

Letter Tracing

Trace the letter below. Color the images that start with the letter O. Color the circles with the letter Oo in them.

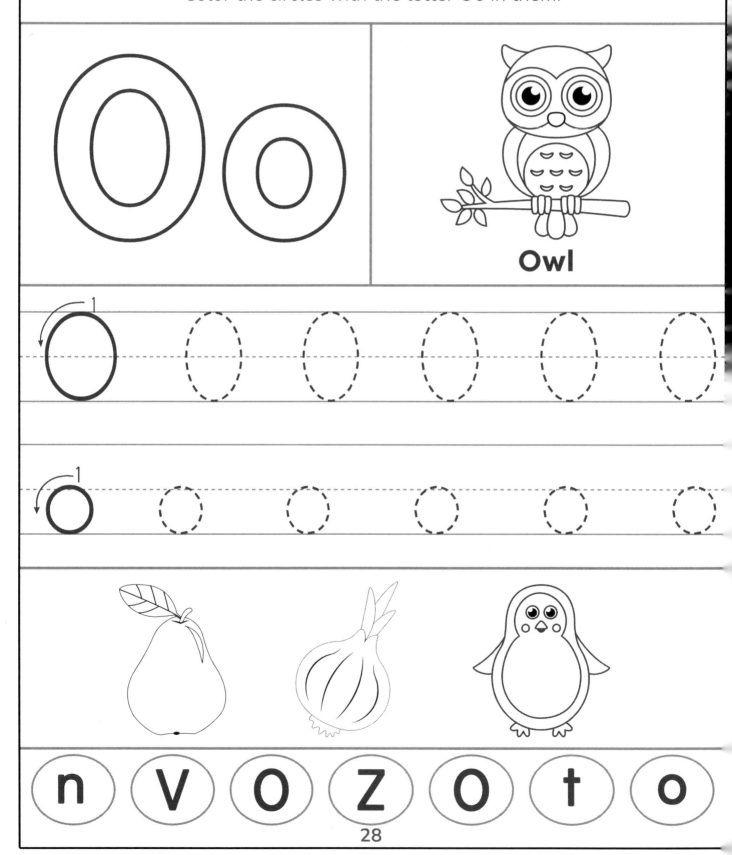

O o

Owl

n v O Z O t o

Letter Tracing

Trace the letter below. Color the images that start with the letter P. Color the circles with the letter Pp in them.

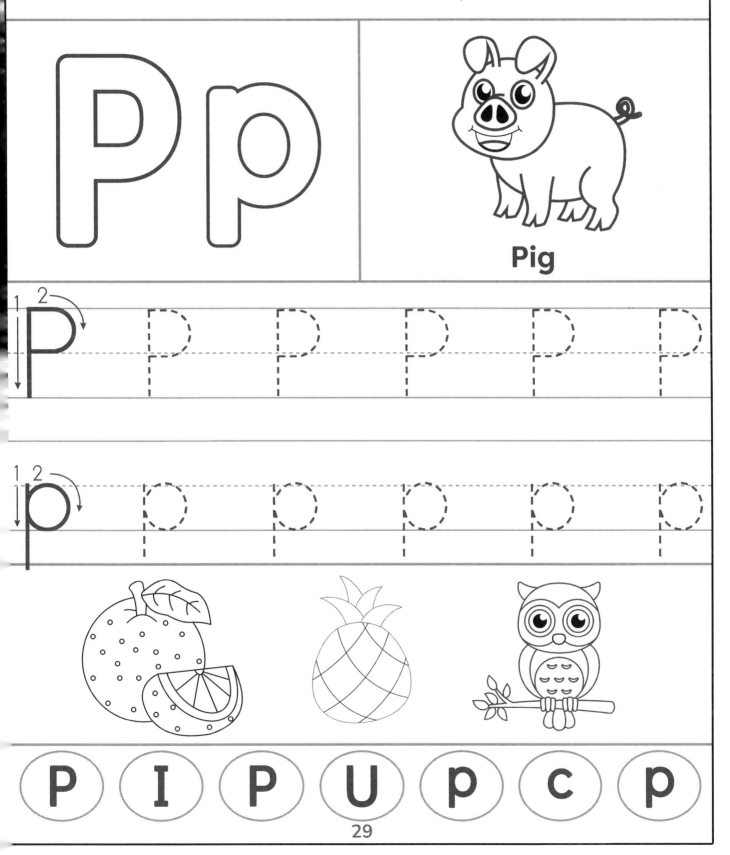

Pig

Letter Tracing

Trace the letter below. Color the images that start with the letter Q.
Color the circles with the letter Qq in them.

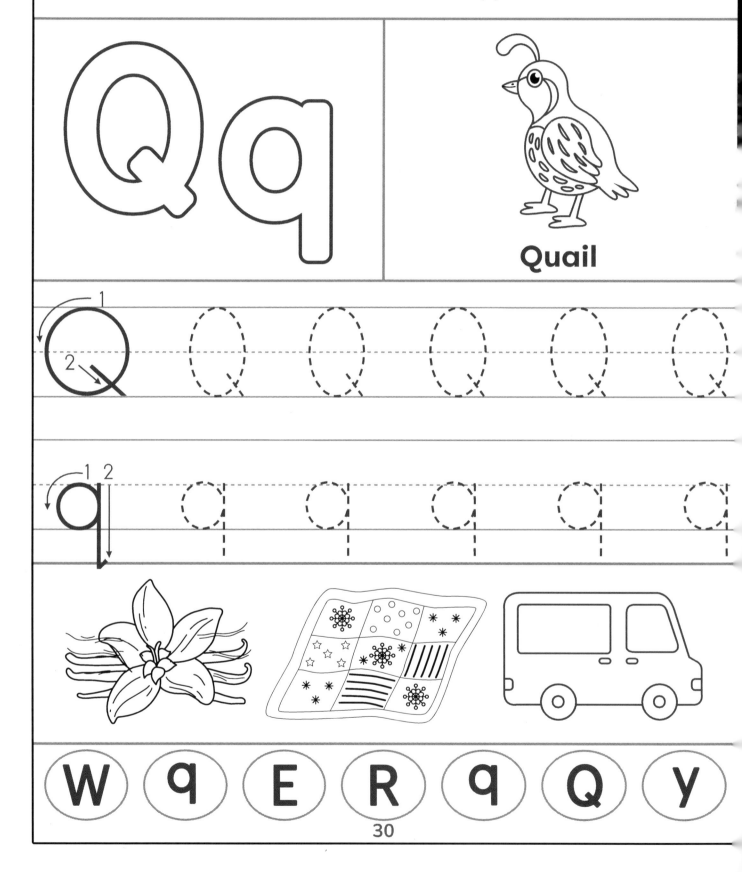

Quail

Letter Tracing

Trace the letter below. Color the images that start with the letter R. Color the circles with the letter Rr in them.

Rabit

R R R R R R

r r r r r r

R F r G r S R

Letter Tracing

Trace the letter below. Color the images that start with the letter S.
Color the circles with the letter Ss in them.

Ship

Trace upper-and lower-case letters T. Trace and read the sentence.
Color the object.

T is for Turtle

Letter Tracing

Trace upper-and lower-case letters U. Trace and read the sentence.
Color the object.

U is for Unicorn

Letter Tracing

Trace upper-and lower-case letters V. Trace and read the sentence.
Color the object.

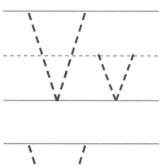

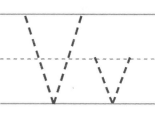

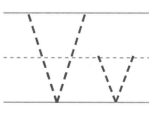

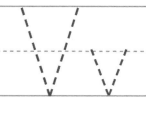

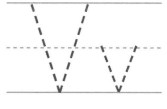

V is for Vulture

Letter Tracing

Trace upper-and lower-case letters W. Trace and read the sentence. Color the object.

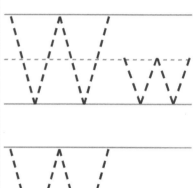

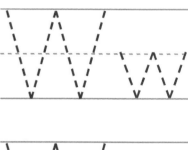

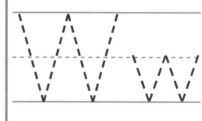

W is for Whale

Letter Tracing

Trace upper-and lower-case letters X. Trace and read the sentence.
Color the object.

X is for Xylophone

Letter Tracing

Trace upper-and lower-case letters Y. Trace and read the sentence.
Color the object.

Y is for Yo-Yo

38

Letter Tracing

Trace upper-and lower-case letters Z. Trace and read the sentence.
Color the object.

Z z

Z is for Zebra

39

Z z

Z z

Z z

Z z

Z z

Z z

A-Z Uppercase Letter

A B C D E F

G H I J K L

M N O P Q R

S T U V W

X Y Z

A-Z Lowercase Letters

a b c d e f

g h i j k l

m n o p q r

s t u v w

x y z

A-z Alphabet

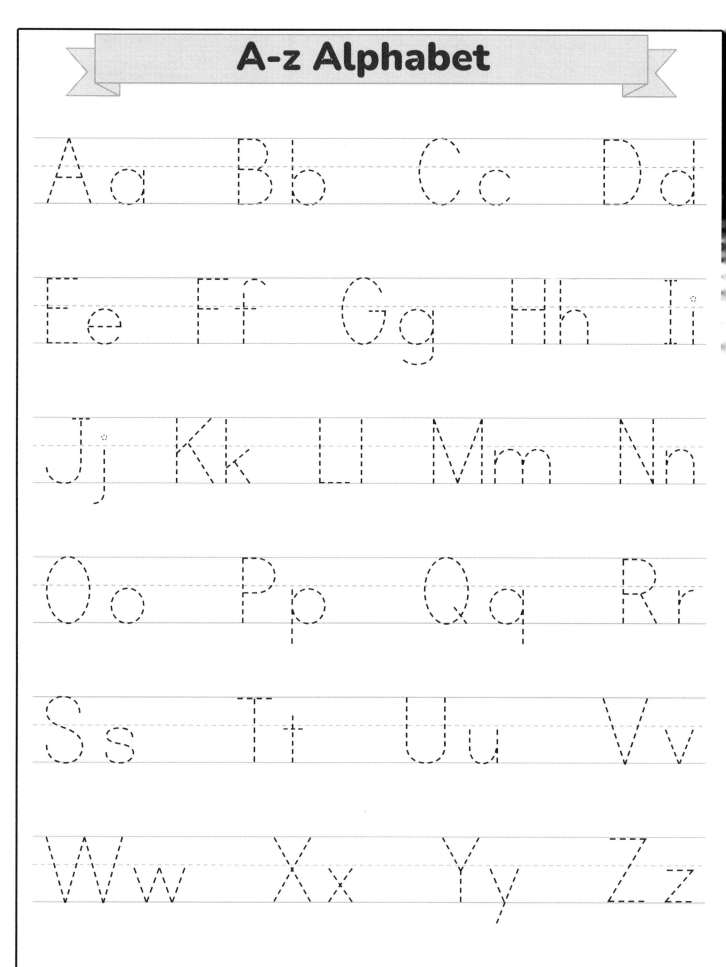

Matching Game

Match the uppercase letter to its lowercase. Color the images.

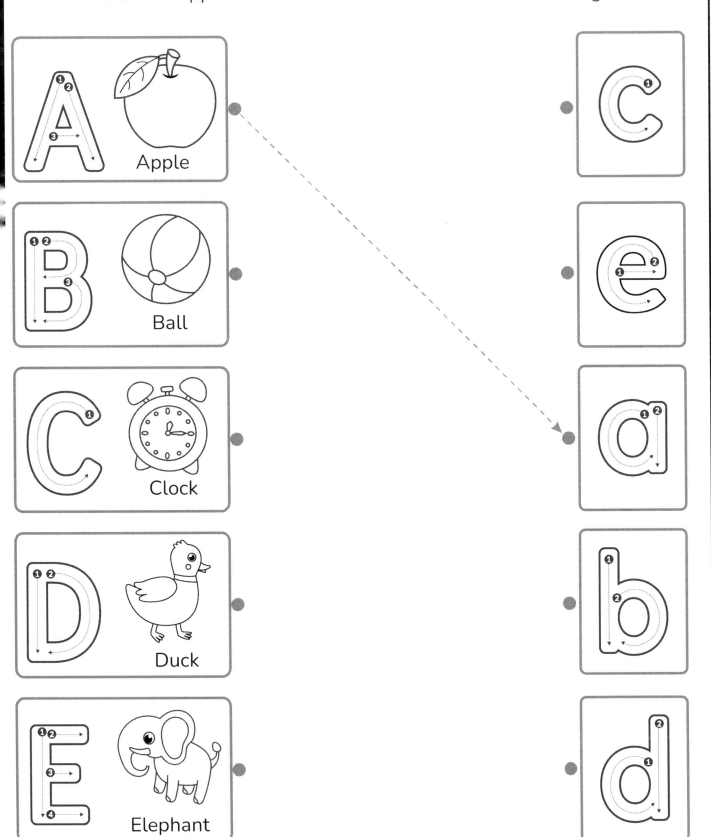

A Apple

B Ball

C Clock

D Duck

E Elephant

c

e

a

b

d

Matching Game

Match the uppercase letter to its lowercase. Color the images.

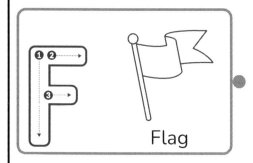
Flag

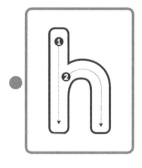

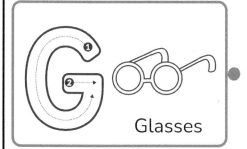
Glasses

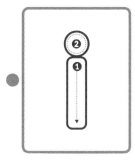

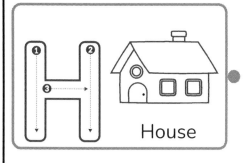
House

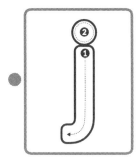

Ice Cream

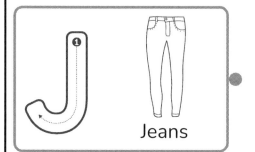
Jeans

Matching Game

Match the uppercase letter to its lowercase. Color the images.

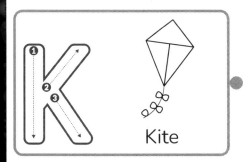

Kite

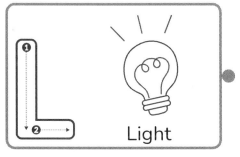

Light

Muffin

Necklace

Owl

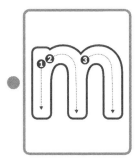

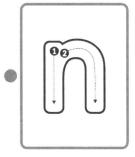

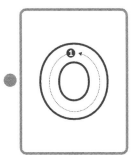

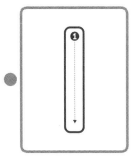

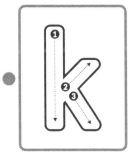

Matching Game

Match the uppercase letter to its lowercase. Color the images.

Penguin

Quail

Rabbit

Star

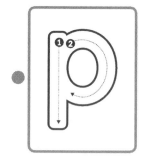

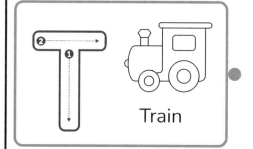

Train

Matching Game

Match the uppercase letter to its lowercase. Color the images.

Unicorn

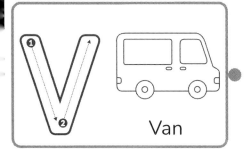
Van

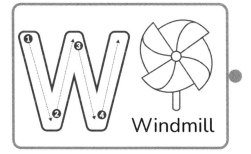
Windmill

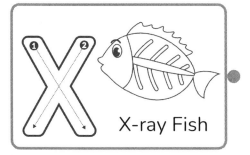
X-ray Fish

Yogurt

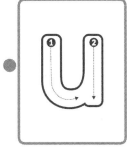

Missing Letters

Fill in the missing uppercase letters.

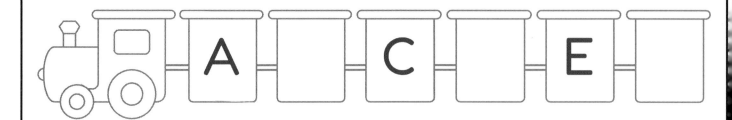
A   C   E

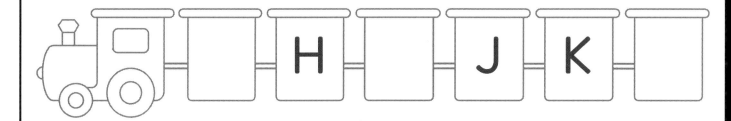
   H   J   K

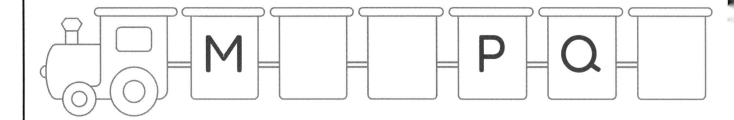
M   P   Q

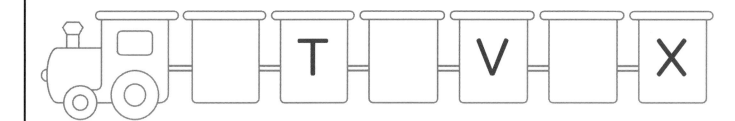
   T   V   X

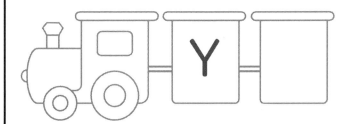
Y

Missing Letters

Fill in the missing lowercase letters.

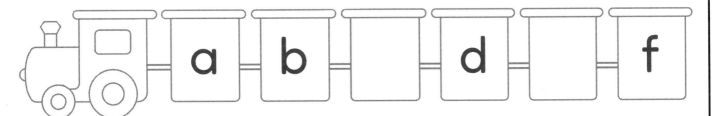

a   b   _   d   _   f

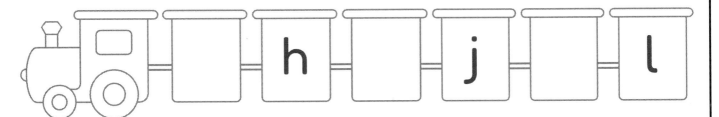

_   h   _   j   _   l

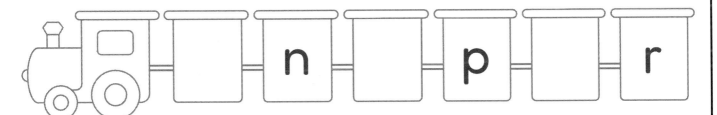

_   n   _   p   _   r

_   _   u   v   _   x

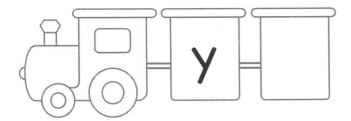

y   _

Number Tracing

Trace the numbers, then write them on your own.

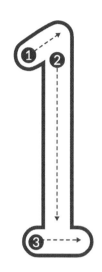

One Goat

Number Tracing

Trace the numbers, then write them on your own.

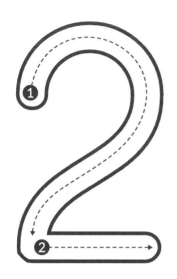

Two Cats

Number Tracing

Trace the numbers, then write them on your own.

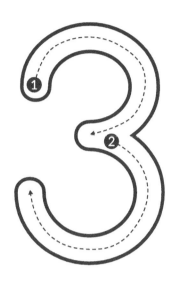

Three Parrots

Number Tracing

Trace the numbers, then write them on your own.

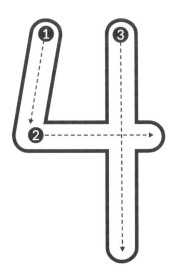

Four Cows

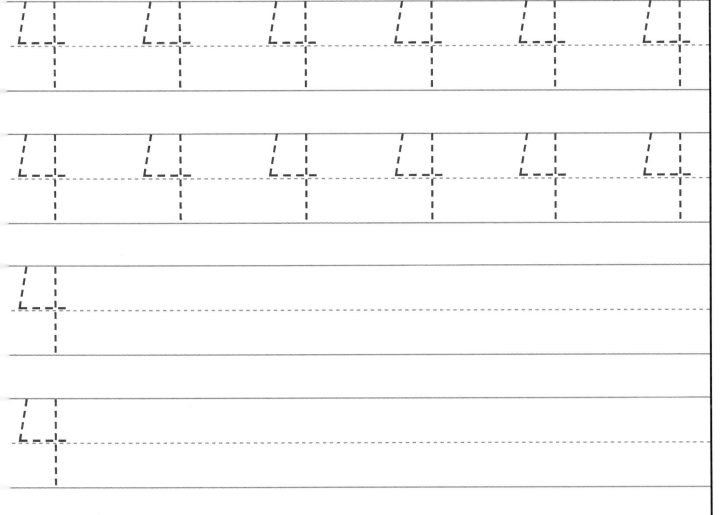

Number Tracing

Trace the numbers, then write them on your own.

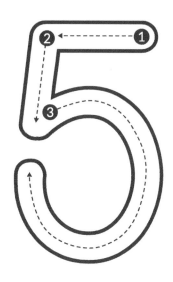

Five Bears

Number Tracing

Trace the numbers, then write them on your own.

Six Unicorns

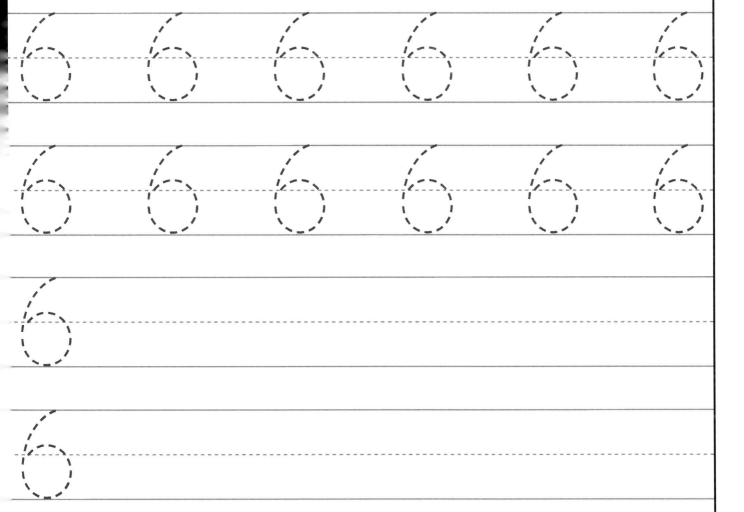

Number Tracing

Trace the numbers, then write them on your own.

Seven Monkeys

Number Tracing

Trace the numbers, then write them on your own.

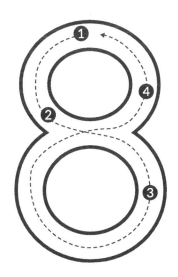

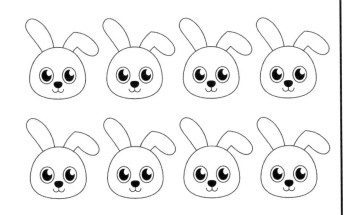

Eight Bunnies

Number Tracing

Trace the numbers, then write them on your own.

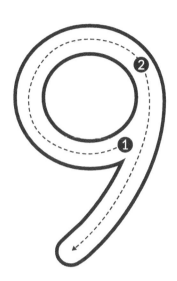

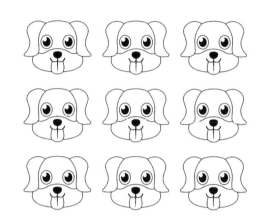

Nine Dogs

Number Tracing

Trace the numbers, then write them on your own.

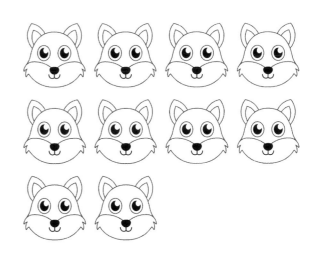

Ten Foxes

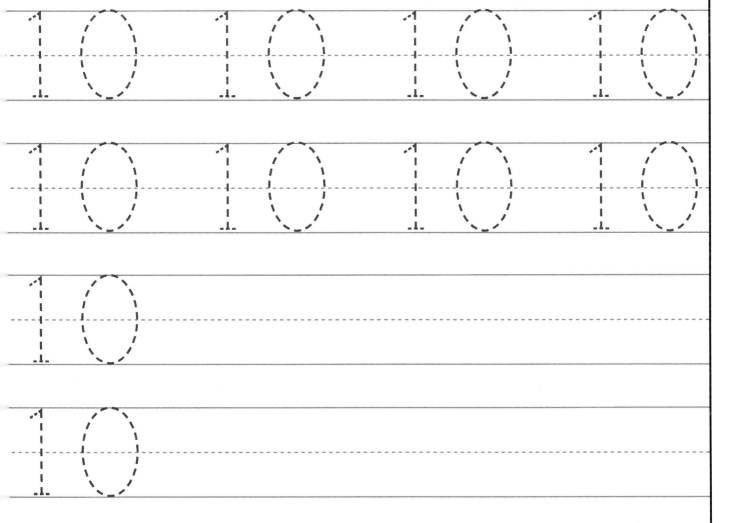

Number Tracing

Trace the numbers, then write them on your own.

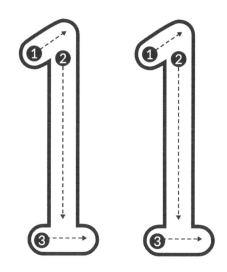

Eleven Giraffes

Number Tracing

Trace the numbers, then write them on your own.

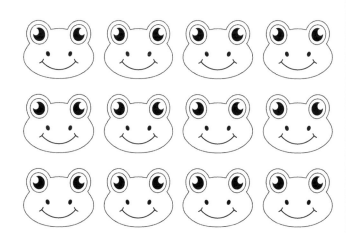

Twelve Frogs

Number Tracing

Trace the numbers, then write them on your own.

Thirteen Ants

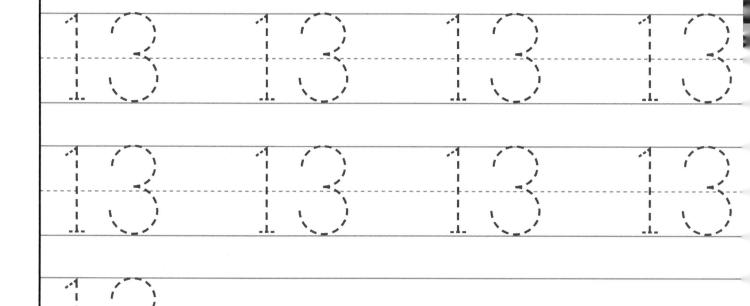

Number Tracing

Trace the numbers, then write them on your own.

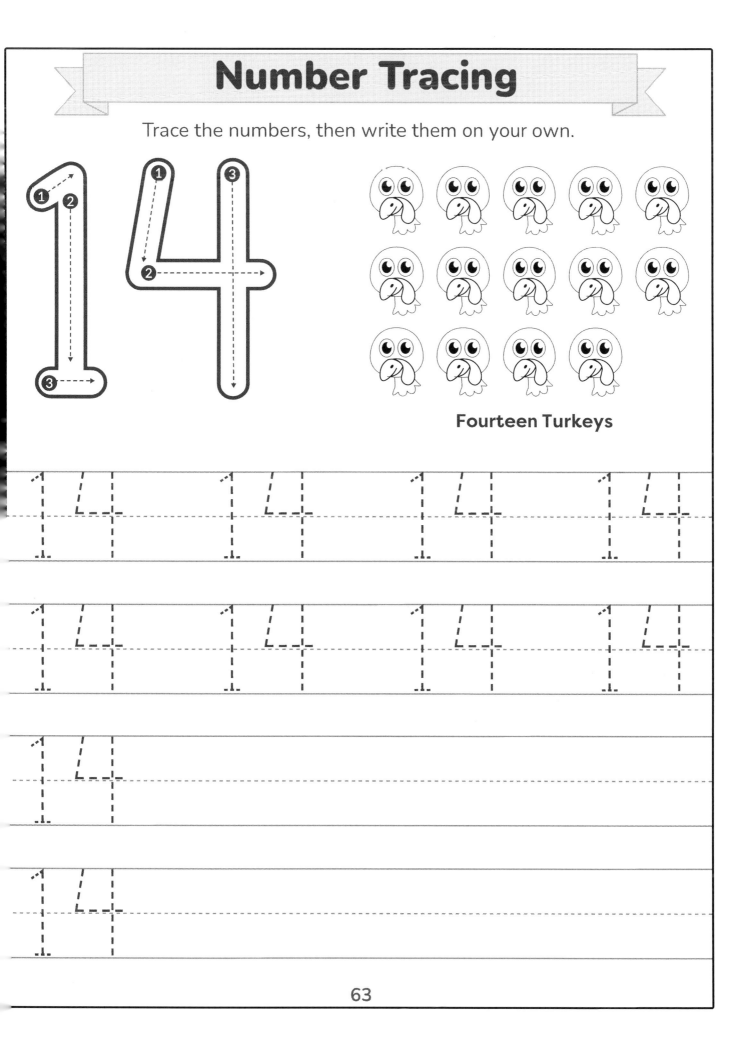

Fourteen Turkeys

Number Tracing

Trace the numbers, then write them on your own.

Fifteen Deers

Number Tracing

Trace the numbers, then write them on your own.

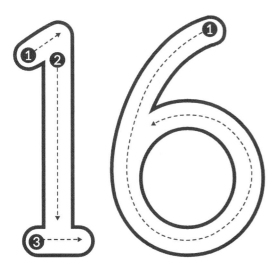

Sixteen Hippos

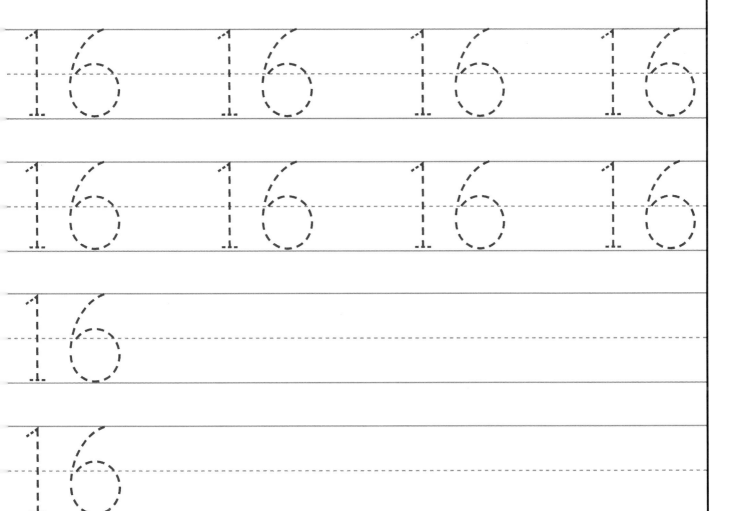

Number Tracing

Trace the numbers, then write them on your own.

Seventeen Hamsters

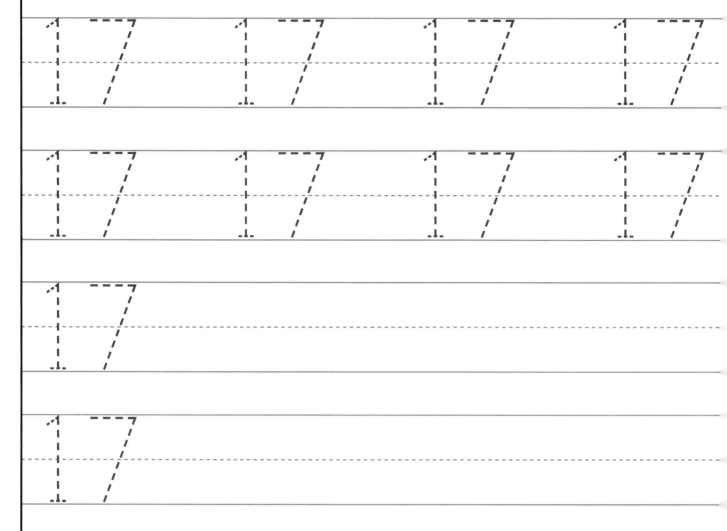

Number Tracing

Trace the numbers, then write them on your own.

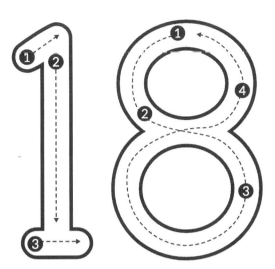

Eighteen Lions

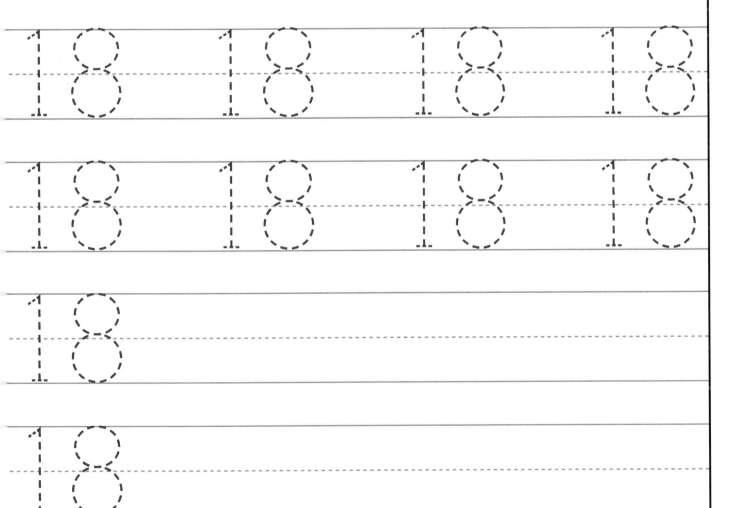

Number Tracing

Trace the numbers, then write them on your own.

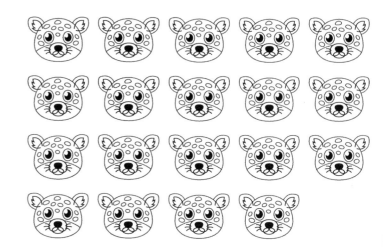

Nineteen Leopards

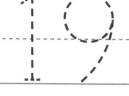   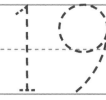

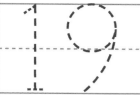 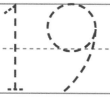  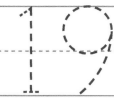

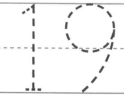

Number Tracing

Trace the numbers, then write them on your own.

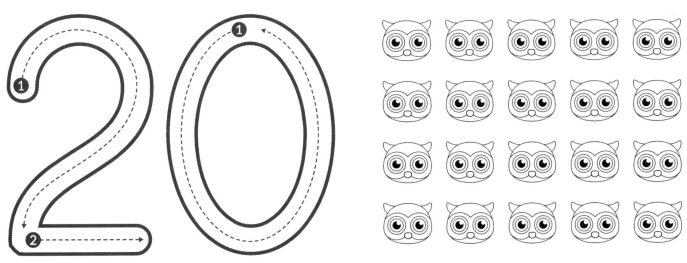

Twenty Owls

Missing Numbers

Fill in the missing numbers.

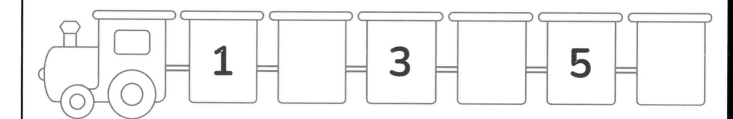

1 □ 3 □ 5 □

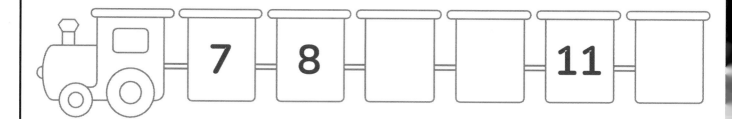

7 8 □ □ 11 □

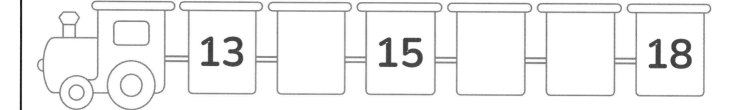

13 □ 15 □ □ 18

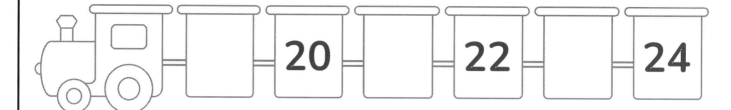

□ 20 □ 22 □ 24

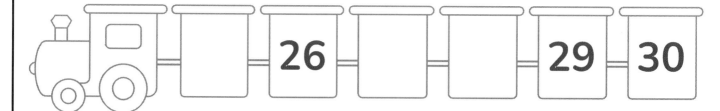

□ 26 □ □ 29 30

70

Count and Color

Trace the number of fish caught in the bucket, then color the amount of fishes.

Count and Color

First, count and color 4 squirrels. Then, count and color 5 nuts.

Color 4 Squirrels

Color 5 Nuts

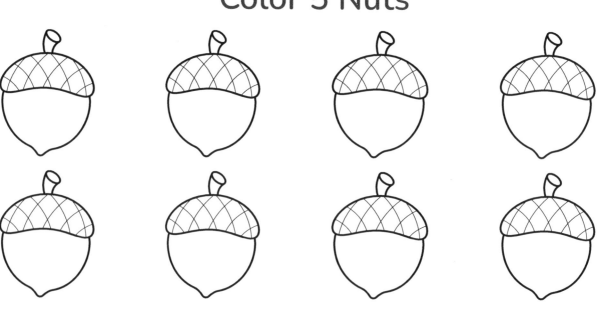

Count and Color

Count the recyclable items in the bins. Then write the number. Color.

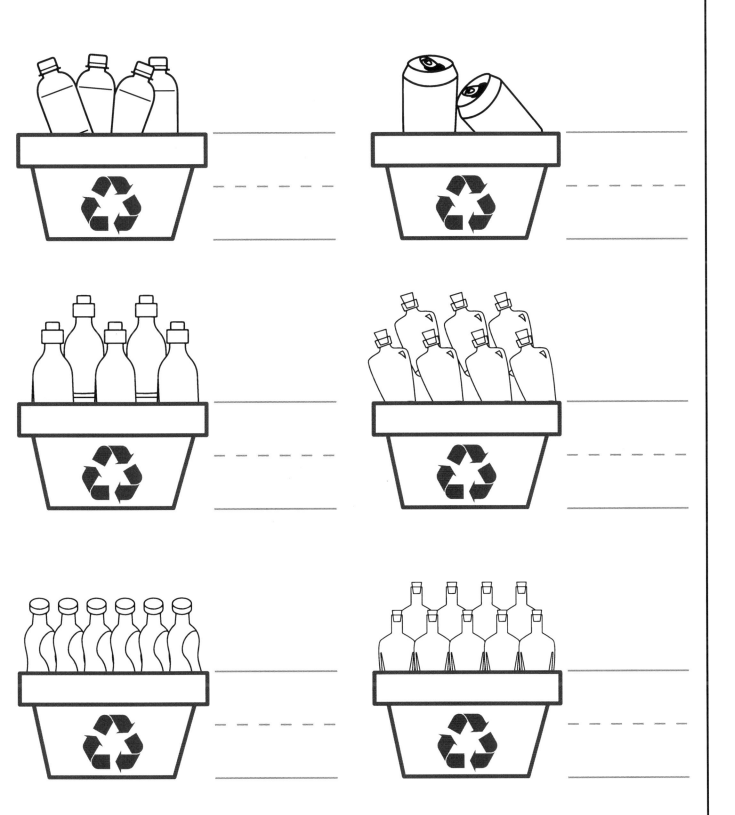

Count and Color

Color the items on the side that has more images.

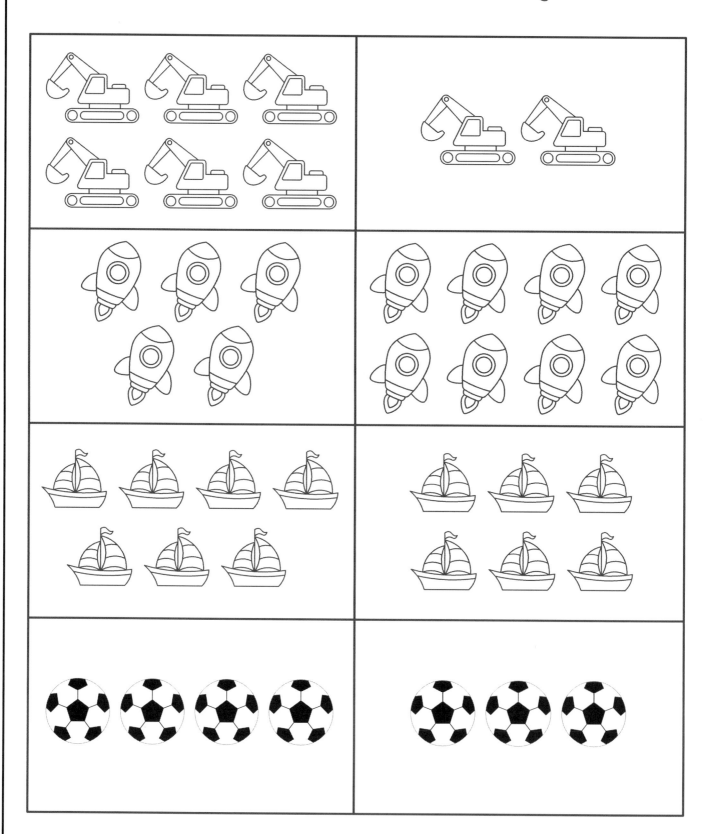

Counting

Color the box that shows the number of objects.

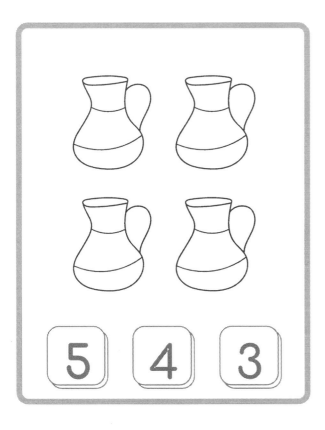

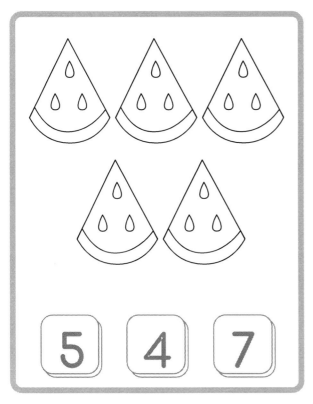

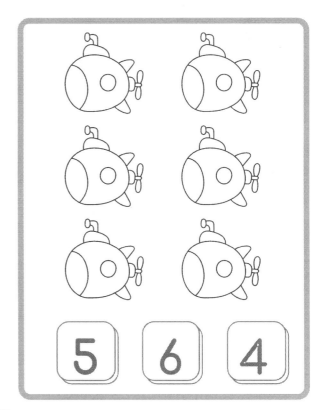

Counting

Color all the numbers 9 in the apple tree.

Counting

Color the box that shows the number of objects.

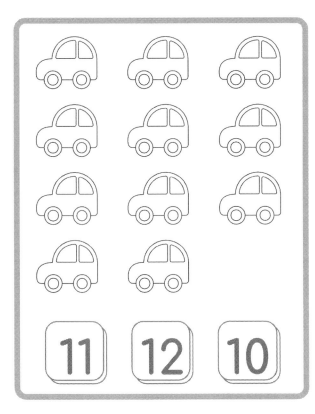

Counting

Color all the numbers 15 in the apple tree.

Numbers Chart

Trace the numbers from 1 to 20 and say them out loud.

1	2	3	4	5
6	7	8	9	10
11	12	13	14	15
16	17	18	19	20

Leave us a Review

Thank You!

Thank you for choosing **Learn to Trace Letter and Numbers.** We hope you and your child enjoyed the activities and had a lot of fun together.

If you find it helpful, please consider leaving a review to share your thoughts. Your feedback helps us improve and assists other parents in finding great resources for their kids. Just scan the QR code below:

SCAN ME

Here are a few questions that can help you guide your review:

- What did you and your child enjoy most about this book?
- How did the activities help your child's learning and development?
- Do you have any suggestions for improvement?

Thank you for your support and for helping us create better books!

Get Free Coloring Pages!

Dear Reader,

Thank you for choosing our book! We would love to stay connected with you and share more exciting content. As a token of our appreciation, we're offering you these FREE coloring pages filled with fun and engaging designs that your kids will love!

How to Get Your Free Coloring Pages:

• Scan the QR code below

• Enter your email address

• Receive and enjoy your free coloring pages!

We look forward to staying in touch and bringing more joy and creativity to your family!

Thank you for your support!

SCAN ME

Certificate of Completion

This certificate is presented to

Learn and Trace The Numbers

GREAT JOB

Date: _____

Sign: _____

Made in United States
Orlando, FL
11 November 2024